Sowing the Seeds of Faith

Inspiration From the Garden of Saints

Amy MacWillliams Schisler
and
Judy MacWilliams

Copyright 2025 Amy Schisler

Cover Photo: Amy Schisler,
The Grotto of Lourdes, Mount St. Mary's University, Emmitsburg, MD
Photo Credits: All photos are copyrighted by and the property of Amy Schisler except:
St. Kateri Tekakwitha: Paige Denton
St. Isadore: Mina Minetto
St. Rose of Lima: Katie Ann Schisler
St. Sebastian, St. Fina, St. Julie Billiart, St. Rose Philippine Duchesne, St. Dorothy, St. Ambrose: Wikicommons, Public Domain

ISBN: 979-8-9900644-5-4

Published by:
Amy Schisler
Bozman, MD 202

$\mathcal{T}$able of contents

"The Saints are friends and models of life for us. Let us invoke them so that they may help us to imitate them and strive to respond generously, as they did, to the divine call." - *His Holiness Benedict XVI*

Introduction

Do you ever wonder about the saints and how they came to be associated with their patronage or their symbols? We hope, through these pocket books, you will gain a greater understanding of the patronage and symbols of the saints.

Why is St. Fiacre the Patron of Gardens and Gardeners? Why does St. Joseph carry a lily? Why is St. Rita of Cascia seen with a rose and figs?

What is a saint?

A saint is someone who has died and gone to Heaven. Some people think a person who goes to Heaven becomes an angel, but this is not so. Angels are not people, but since they are in Heaven, we can say they are saints, like St. Michael or St. Gabriel.

So, what is the difference between someone you know who has died and someone like St. Patrick or St. Luke or St. Teresa of Calcutta? In the Early Church, saints were declared by popular proclamation, typically because they were martyred. Since the 10th Century, the Catholic Church has announced sainthood based on a thorough, four-step vetting process.

After a person dies, a request is made to the Vatican making a case to canonize said person. Once a case is formally opened, the *Congregation for the Causes of the Saints* at the Vatican rigorously investigates the person's life. If the person is deemed to have lived an extraordinarily holy life, he or she may be declared *"venerable."*

If a person gave his or her life for Christ and died for Him, he or she is called a martyr and may be *"beatified"* and named *"blessed"* without any further investigation. If he or she was not martyred, people may pray to the person asking for a miracle to occur. If miracles are scientifically proven as having no other explanation, the person may be *"canonized"* and declared a saint.

After all these things happen, the Pope announces the person is holy and is in Heaven, interceding on our part and praying for us. People may pray to that saint for intercession or guidance. Churches, schools, and other places or organizations may be named after the saint.

The Church does not create saints. It announces that God has made the person a saint by granting them entry to Heaven. Many saints are patrons, meaning they, with the permission of God, may assist certain people or places with their needs or may be called upon for intercession in that area.

An intercession is prayer we send through someone else for help. It's like asking a friend to mail a letter for you since they are already going to the post office. Saints are in Heaven with God and are close to Him. They can talk to Him and ask Him to help us. It's like asking the mother to help a child convince the father to give the child something he or she wants. The child can ask the father, and he or she should, but the mother can help him make his decision. Everything we ask, if we are praying to the saints, should be asked in the name of Jesus.

Canonized saints are given patronages, people, places, or things that they protect or for which they specifically intervene. There are patrons of places (Our Lady of the Immaculate Conception is the patroness of the United States, and Our Lady of Guadalupe is the patroness of Latin America). There are patrons of animals (St. Francis, or St. Roch, the patron of dogs). There are patrons of occupations (St. Thomas Aquinas is the patron of attorneys, and St. John Baptist de La Salle is the patron of teachers).

4

Saints are always there for us, ready to take our prayers to Jesus just like we are always there for our friends and family to help them with their needs. When you pray for someone on earth, you are being just like the saints in Heaven.

Saints Associated With Flowers

St. Joseph – The Lily
(30 B.C. – 20 A.D.)

Patron of families, fathers, immigrants, workers, a happy death, the Universal Church, and many others

According to a tradition from the earliest days of the Church, the child, Mary, was consecrated to God as promised by her parents.

In visions given to Blessed Anne Catherine Emmerich by Mary herself, Mary left the temple at 14 to be married, even though she was a consecrated virgin.* In a revelation from God, she was reminded of the verse, "*And here shall come forth a rod out of the root of Jesse; and a flower shall rise up out of his root*" (Is 11:1).

Men from the line of David were

presented to Mary in the temple, and each was handed a branch to lay on the altar. When Joseph attempted to place his branch on the altar, a white lily blossomed from it, thus letting Mary know that Joseph was the man chosen for her by God.

Dear St. Joseph,
Help me to listen to God, to seek His revelations, and to choose wisely in the garden of life. Amen.

You can read more about the visions Blessed Anne Catherine received from Mary in her book, The Life of the Blessed Virgin Mary.

St. Mary – Impatiens
(22 B.C. - A.D. 41)

Patron of countries, dioceses, and places around the world; nuns, aviators, the sick, young women, motherhood, childbirth, and more

Impatiens are small flowers which produce an abundance of seeds that travel by capsules and can end up several miles away from their mother plant.

The smallest flowers of this family are referred to as *Our Lady's Earrings* and represent Mary's faith and trust in God. At the Visitation, Elizabeth proclaimed about Mary, "Blessed is she who believed that there would be a fulfillment of what was spoken to her by the Lord" (Luke 1:45). Mary believed the words of God and acted upon them entirely on faith, always attentive to His call and the call of His Son.

Mary is the Mother of all Christians, the model disciple and first Christian. Like impatiens, the seeds of her love and faithfulness extend far and wide. Her intercessory nature sows seeds of trust and comfort among those seeking her aid.

Dear Mother Mary,
Take me into your maternal care,
and help me to incline my ear toward the voice of God, always open to His call, ever obedient to His commands. Amen.

St. Mary – The Rose
(22 B.C. - A.D. 41)

The rose is the symbol of purity, beauty, and love. It is considered the most noble of flowers, requiring close care in gardens though it grows wild in nature. It can be found in many colors and fragrances. What better flower is there to associate with Mary?

Mary is seen as the Rose of Sharon in the Song of Solomon. The closed petal rose symbolizes her virginity, and the rose windows of many Gothic cathedrals represent Mary. Our Lady of Guadalupe performed the miracle of the roses to convince the Bishop to believe Juan Diego's visions of her.

Mary's Psalter, a collection of prayers and meditations on the lives of Mary and Jesus, is often characterized as a garden of prayers, in Latin, a *rosarium*. We know it better as The Rosary.

Dear Mother Mary,
Help me to be pure in love and noble in
action, growing my world with care
and love.
Amen.

St. John the Baptist – Hypericum
(St. John's Wort) (4 B.C. – 30 A.D.)

Patron of monks, tailors, hermits, converts, prisoners, and epileptics

St John's Wort, as it is known today, has been around for centuries under the name, hypericum. It was believed to be a talisman which kept away evil spirits and cured those thought to be possessed. It was burned in the Midsummer's Eve bonfires, lit to dispel demons.

During the Church's efforts to eliminate pagan customs and rituals during the Dark Ages, June 24, was designated as the Feast of St. John the Baptist, and the flower became associated with the saint instead of the pagan ritual.

The Church taught that the flower, newly named the *Plant (Wort) of St. John*, symbolized the sun which dispels darkness. St. John heralded the coming of the Light of the World.

It is believed that the demons who possessed individuals cured by drinking hypericum tea were most likely suffering from depression. Thus, the plant's healing properties were more fact than fiction!

Dear St. John,
May your
proclamation of the
coming of the SON
light all my days.
Am en.

St. Sebastian – The Palm Branch

(256-287)

Patron of athletes, soldiers, and martyrs

The legend of St. Sebastian tells of a young man who became a Roman soldier to spread the word about Christ among the army. When found to be a Christian, he was arrested and condemned to death by the Emperor Diocletian.

The soldiers, following Diocletian's orders, shot Sebastian several times with arrows. One account said he was "full of arrows as an urchin." Found in the woods by Irene, wife of another martyr, Sebastian was still alive. She took him to her home and nursed him until he regained his strength.

Once recovered, Sebastian sought out the emperor and accused him of cruelty to Christians. This time, Sebastian's arrest resulted in his death after being beaten with clubs.

Sebastian is depicted riddled with arrows and sometimes seen with a palm branch, the symbol of martyrdom.

Dear St. Sebastian,
Even when faced with death, you
continued to preach
about Christ. Be my
protector and
soldier, encouraging
me to have no fear
when I would cower
rather than
speaking out for
what is right. Amen.

St. Aedan – Fern

(550-632)

Patron of Ferns, Ireland

St. Aedan (also known as St. Maedoc) was born on the isle of Breaghwy in County Cavan. While still a child, he was taken hostage by the High King of Ireland, Ainmire. So impressed with the boy was the king, that he offered to release him, but Aedan refused to leave unless all the king's prisoners were set free.

Aedan studied at Saint Finnian at Clonard Abbey and grew to be known for his sanctity and devotion to religious life. He made his way to Wales to study under St. David and became one of the saints most trusted disciples.

In 570, he returned home with several hives of honeybees which were scarce on the island. He was given a vast amount of land to be used to build a monastery. He built his first church and monastery in Ferns, Ireland and was heralded for his kindness and generosity.

St. Aedan is buried beneath the Cathedral in Ferns, Ireland.

Dear St. Aedan,
It's not easy always being kind and generous, but you were looked up to for those qualities. Help me to be kind and generous to all those I encounter, especially those who keep me imprisoned by their own desires. Amen.

St. Clare – The Lily
(1194-1253)

Patron of eye disease, embroiderers, laundry workers, and television

One can't think of St. Clare without recalling St. Francis of Assisi. The two are linked by their shared hometown, mutual love of God, religious orders, and loving friendship and support of each other.

Francis grew up in the wealthy part of Assisi, and Clare lived her childhood as a peasant, but they found kinship in their great love for God and desire to found religious orders to serve Him. After founding the Franciscans, Francis aided Clare in forming the Poor Clares, modeled after most of the Franciscan tenets. She referred to herself as *"The little plant of Francis."* While dying,

Clare was able to "watch" Francis's funeral through a miraculous vision on the wall of her room.

While it's true that Francis helped Clare get her start, she blossomed on her own with God's grace. She and her order grew and flourished just as the lilies in the fields.

Dear St. Clare,
Rather than run from your poverty, you embraced it and used your means to
help the poor of
Assisi. Help me to
embrace those
things that weigh
me down and see
them as means to
glorify God. Amen.

St. Fina – Violets
(1238-1253)

Patron of those with physical disabilities

Seraphina, known affectionately as St. Fina, was born in San Geminiano, Italy to parents who had fallen into poverty. She was a child of great beauty who, though she was poor, always gave half her food to those worse off than herself.

Fina spent her days sewing and spinning yarn and much of her nights in prayer. Around the time of her father's death, Fina was plagued by a series of illnesses that left her paralyzed and caused failure of her internal organs. Once a lovely maiden, she lost her beauty to the disease. For six years, she lay on a wooden plank, determined to align her sufferings with the Crucified Christ. She spent hours repeating, "It is not my wounds but thine, O Christ, that hurt me."

With the sudden death of her mother, Fina became dependent upon the poor who once depended upon her. After her death, her body was removed from the plank, which was found to be covered with white violets.

Dear St. Fina,
Oh, how you suffered, but you used your suffering to grow closer to Christ. Help me to suffer with dignity, my eyes always on the Lord. Amen.

St. Rita of Cascia– The Rose
(1386-1457)

Patron of parenthood, infertility, difficult marriages, impossible causes

Rita was born and raised in Roccaporena, Italy. She was a wife, mother, and widow who became a nun after the deaths of her husband and sons.

Known for her charity and prayer life, Rita developed wounds in her forehead that were compared to the wounds from the Crown of Thorns. She mediated frequently on Christ's passion, tended to the sick and poor, and counseled those who sought her advice.

Rita is known as the *Saint of the Rose* and is often depicted with figs and a rose due to the story that at the time her death, she asked that two figs and a rose be brought to her from the garden of her childhood home. Though it was late in winter, Rita's cousin went to the garden and found a rose and two figs lying in the snow.

The finding of the rose in winter led to St. Rita, with St. Jude, being known as a patron of impossible causes.

Dear St. Rita,
I come to you when all hope seems lost.
Please pray for my
needs and for
acceptance of God's
will. Amen.

St. Kateri Tekakwitha – The Lily
(1656-1680)

Patron of ecology and the environment

Born Tekakwitha, St. Kateri was a Mohawk woman who converted to Christianity after a tragic childhood. She lost her parents and brother to smallpox, brought to America by slave traders. Tekakwitha survived and was adopted by her aunt and uncle, but the pocks left behind severely scarred her face.

Around the age of eleven, Tekakwitha encountered Jesuit missionaries who taught her about Christ and the Catholic faith. At seventeen, she was to be forced into marriage but fled her village and found shelter with Jesuit missionaries and told them of her desire to become a Christian.

Tekakwitha took the name Kateri after St. Catherine of Siena. She always maintained her Mohawk love of the earth and closeness to nature. She spent much time in the woods talking to and listening for God. She is known as the *Lily of the Mohawks.*

Dear St. Kateri,
Help me find God in all things of nature.
Remind me to always seek Him in the beauty of the earth, sea, and sky, knowing He created the world and all its splendor just as he created me. A men.

St. Julie Billiart – The Sunflower
(1751-1816)

Patron of educators and teachers

Julie Billiart was born in France to a well-off farming family. From an early age, she showed interest in religion and helping the poor and sick. She grew up working on the farm but spent her spare time catechizing children and other farm workers. At the age of 30, she was mysteriously paralyzed for twenty years. She taught catechism from her bed and acted as a spiritual advisor.

Despite her pain, she aided fugitive priests in the French Revolution. She was smuggled to Compiegne and hidden from the soldiers. It was during this time that she received a vision of the order she was to begin.

In 1803, Julie and Françoise Blin de Bourdon, established the Institute of Notre Dame and the Sisters of Notre Dame, dedicated to educating poor girls and training catechists. At this same time, Julie walked for the first time in twenty-two years. She encouraged the sisters to *"Be like the sunflower that follows every movement of the sun, and keep your eyes always turned towards our good God."*

Dear St. Julie,
Help me to always
follow the SON and
turn toward God.
Amen.

St. Rose Philippine Duchesne – Hawthorn Blossoms

(1769-1852)

Patron of families, fathers, immigrants, workers, a happy death, the Universal Church, and many others.

Named by the Potawatomi Indians, *Woman Who Always Prays*, St. Rose Philippine Duchesne was a French sister, baptized with the names of St. Philip the Apostle and St. Rose of Lima.

Throughout her life, Rose felt called to be a missionary. In 1818, she was sent to the Louisiana Territory to help the bishop educate and evangelize the Native and French children in the territory. She founded six schools in Missouri and Louisiana and aided in beginning a school for Native American children in Kansas.

Rose is associated with hawthorn blossoms, the symbol of hope. No matter the circumstances, Rose was a consummate optimist and brought a sense of unwavering hope to everyone around her.

Dear St. Rose,
Life can be hard. Sometimes, I feel so defeated. Help me, always, to have hope and to see goodness everywhere. Amen.

The Legend of the Dogwood

-Author Unknown

In Jesus time, the dogwood grew
To a stately size and a lovely hue.
'Twas strong & firm it's branches interwoven
For the cross of Christ its timbers were
chosen.
Seeing the distress at this use of their wood
Christ made a promise which still holds
good:
"Never again shall the dogwood grow
Large enough to be used so
Slender & twisted, it shall be
With blossoms like the cross for all to see.
As blood stains the petals marked in brown
The blossom's center wears a throny crown.
All who see it will remember me
Crucified on a cross from the dogwood tree.
Cherished and protected this tree shall be
A reminder to all of my agony."

Saints Associated With Occupations

St. Dorothy – Gardeners
(279-311)

Patron of gardeners

A resident of Caesarea in Cappadocia, Dorothy lived during the reign of Diocletian, a time of Christian persecution. Dorothy, a perpetual virgin, considered herself a bride of Christ. She often spoke with joy about "the garden" she would soon be able to live in, referring to Paradise with the Lord. On her way to her execution, Dorothy was mocked by a young lawyer, Theophilus, to send her fruits and flowers when she reached her garden.

There are two accounts of what happened next. An angel appeared to Dorothy, holding a basket of three apples and three roses (three being the Biblical representation of the presence of God). Dorothy sent the basket to Theophilus, telling him she would meet him in the garden.

In another telling, a young boy was sent to him with Dorothy's headdress, which radiated the scent of apples and roses. In both cases, Theophilus then converted to Christianity and was executed.

Dear St. Dorothy,
Pray for me throughout my life and at the hour of my death that I may join you in the Heavenly garden. Amen.

St. Ambrose of Milan – Beekeepers
(339-397)

Patron of beekeepers, bees, and candlemakers

One of the greatest bishops in the Church's history, St. Ambrose was born in Trier, Germany but served as Bishop of Milan. A legend tells of Ambrose being swarmed by bees as a child. Though they flew into his face and surrounded his head, he was not stung even once. They did leave behind drops of honey on his face. Perhaps the bees appreciated his name—Ambrosia is Latin for honey!

Later, as a priest and theologian, Ambrose was known as the *honey-tongued doctor* due to his eloquent speaking. He was a friend and spiritual advisor to St. Monica.

Ambrose was a great defender of the Church and stood on his belief that the Church was independent of the crown and could not be told what to do by the emperors. Perhaps St. Ambrose is most famous for the being influential in the conversion of St. Augustine.

Dear St. Ambrose,
May I always remember that God's love for me is as sweet as honey. May my own faith serve to sweeten the lives of those around me and be influential in their journeys of faith. Amen.

St. Benedict – Agricultural Workers
(480-547)

Patron of agricultural workers, civil engineers, cave explorers, religious orders, and those suffering from gall stones, fever, kidney disease, and inflammatory disorders, as well as against poisoning.

St. Benedict, founder of many monastic orders, was born in Rome. His sister, Scholastica, was his closest friend and also founded a number of religious orders.

As part of the Rule of Benedict (which still governs the lives of monks), Benedict expected monks to do physical labor dedicated to God. Contrary to the norms of Roman life, he did not believe in being idle and was adamant that his followers be able to provide for themselves through the work of their hands.

Many of his monks cultivated gardens and engaged in other productive works. Today, brewing beer, producing wine, and cultivating other items from produce, such as honey and jams, are often among the primary means of support for monks.

Dear St. Benedict,
Help me in my everyday tasks to dedicate all that I do to God and to go about my work with diligence and humility. Amen.

St. Fiacre – Gardeners
(600-670)

Patron of growers of vegetables, medicinal plants, and gardens

Fiacre was born in Ireland but left for France, hoping to live as a hermit, dedicating his life to prayer. When he arrived, the Bishop (St. Faro) offered him as much land as he could till in a day. Rather than use a plow, Fiacre began tilling with his priest's staff. In one day, he cleared such a large tract of land of trees and shrubs and tilled so much earth, it could only be called a miracle.

On his land, Fiacre cultivated gardens, built himself a small cell in which to live, and built a chapel in honor of the Blessed Virgin Mary.

Though he sought a life of solitude, many went to him to be cured. The stories of his miraculous healings abound, especially his ability to dismiss a particular tumor, still known today as the Tumor of Fiacre.

Dear St. Fiacre,
Pray for me, that I may till the gardens of life to produce good works in the name of the Lord. Amen.

St. Ansovinus –Agriculture
(Died 868)

Patron of agriculture and the protection of crops

Ansovinus, was born in Camerino, Italy where he eventually became Bishop. He entered religious life at a young age and lived many years as a hermit. Before being elected as Bishop, he served as a counselor to Louis II, the Holy Roman Emperor.

Many miracles have been attributed to Ansovinus regarding his inexplicable ability to feed those in need. One story tells that he was able to produce an endless amount of food in a very small cooking pot and fed every person that came to him seeking food. On another occasion, Ansovinus was able to feed hundreds, perhaps even thousands, of people from a single granary. When he was told that the grain had run out, he sent his helpers to check again, and the granary was miraculously filled to capacity.

Dear St. Ansovinus,
As human beings, we tend to be selfish
and want to keep everything to
ourselves. Help me to seek ways to share
with others, especially when I am blessed
with a bounty of food. Amen.

St. Isadore – Farmers
(1170-1133)

Patron of farmers, peasants, day laborers, agriculture, and bricklayers

Isadore entered life as servant when he was still a child. He farmed the fields of a wealthy landowner, Juan de Vargas, his entire life. He and his wife (St. Maria de la Cabeza) lived a simple life as farmers and servants of God.

Isadore was a daily Mass devotee, and he spent his days off visiting churches in and around Madrid. As he plowed the fields, he prayed, enjoying long dialogues with God. He and Maria shared all that they had with the poor.

There are many miraculous stories about angels plowing the fields while Isadore prayed. Once, when he brought home many people seeking food, the pot of soup Maria made sustained everyone though she had only made enough for two.

Isadore lies at rest with St. Maria in the Church of St. Isadore in Spain. His body is incorrupt.

Dear St. Isadore,
Guide me in my daily labors so that all the seeds I plant may bear fruit. Amen.

St. Rose of Viterbo– Flower Growers
(1235-1252)

Patron of flower growers and florists

Even as a child, Rose's desire was to pray and live as a recluse. When she was just three years old, she raised her aunt from the dead. After an illness brought her near death herself, the Virgin Mary appeared to Rose and cured her.

Rose wore her name well. She was said to have bloomed like a rose in the Church's garden before being transplanted to Paradise.[1]

Many miracles were attributed to the young girl. Once, she was discovered by her father taking the family's food to the

---

[1] https://www.roman-catholic-saints.com/saint-rose-of-viterbo.html

poor. When ordered to show what she had, she opened her apron, and fragrant roses were there instead.

Rose longed to enter St. Mary of the Roses Monastery, but she was refused because of her poverty. She died at the age of 17 and remains in Viterbo, where her body is incorrupt.

Dear St. Rose,
May the seeds of my life flower in God's garden, giving glory to Him always, as you did. Amen.

St. Rose of Lima– Flower Growers and Gardeners
(1586-1617)

Patron of gardeners, flower growers, and embroiderers

Rose was born in Lima, Peru, at the time of the first wave of evangelization of South America. She was so bothered by her own beauty, she rubbed her face with pepper and wore a crown of metal thorns to make herself humble.

Rose spent all day creating fine lace and embroidered items to sell to make money for her family and for the poor. At night, she gardened by moonlight, growing food to support her family.

Rose's parents wanted her to marry, to bring money into the family, but she refused. Since they would not let her join a convent, she joined the Third Order of the Franciscans and lived a life of solitude.

In the last years of her life, Rose established the social service system in Peru by taking in the homeless, elderly, and sick.

Dear St. Rose,
Help me to see my skills as gifts from the Lord and to use them to help those around me and to care for God's people. Amen.

St. Thérèse of Lisieux – Florists
(1871-1897)

Patron Saint of florists, foreign missions, loss of parents, priests, and the sick

St. Thérèse was a 19th Century French girl who became a nun at 15. She lived according to her *Little Way*, a belief that everyone can perform small acts of love to give glory to God. She thought of herself as *The Little Flower of Jesus* and believed flowers were created to give God glory.

In her book, *Story of a Soul*, St. Thérèse wrote of snow, *"While I was still quite small, its whiteness entranced me...Perhaps it was because, being a little winter flower, my eyes first saw the earth clad in its beautiful white mantle."* On the January day she entered the convent, she hoped for snow, but the weather was more like spring. Upon taking her vows, she turned toward the courtyard, and to the everyone's amazement, it was covered in snow.

Snowdrops are the first flowers of spring, often blooming when there is still snow on the ground. Like the flower, Thérèse found love in despair, light in darkness, and life even in the throes of death.

Dear St. Thérèse,
Help me to give glory to God by doing small things with great love. Amen.

Symbolism of Flowers in the Catholic Faith

"Consider the lilies of the field, how they grow: they labor not, neither do they spin. But I say to you, that not even Solomon in all his glory was arrayed as one of these" (Matt. 6: 28-29).

Flowers have long served as symbols in the Catholic faith. According to St. Jerome, flowers have adorned the altar since the earliest days of the Church.[2] Many of these flowers are steeped in symbolism, and a large number of saints may be associated with various flowers.

Carnation – Carnations often decorate churches during weddings, as they are symbols of love and marriage. They also symbolize perfect obedience. Saints represented by carnations are:
Mary
St. Joan of Arc

Columbine – These small blue and purple

---

[2] Jerome's Letter to Heliodorus, Letter 60

flowers represent the victory of life over death and are associated with humility, the Holy Spirit, and the Holy Trinity.

Clover – The clover represents the Holy Trinity. Saints:
St. Patrick

Daisy – Daisies came into use in churches in the 15th Century to represent the innocence of the Christ Child. Saints:
Mary
St. Michael

Fern – Ferns symbolize solitary, humility, honesty, and sincerity. Saints:
St. Aedan (aka St. Maedoc)

Hyacinth – The hyacinth represents the Christian virtue of prudence as well as peace of mind, and the desire for Heaven. Saints:
St. Hyacinth
St. Valentine

Holly – Holly has long been associated with Christ's Crown and Thorns and His Passion.

Saints:
St. John the Baptist

Hypericum – Hypericum blooms between June and August, often beginning around June 24, the feast day of John the Baptist. Saints: St. John the Baptist

Impatiens – These flowers are referred to as *Our Lady's Earrings* and represent Mary and her faith and trust in God and His Word.

Iris – Iris means *sword lily* and symbolizes Our Mother of Sorrows.

Lady Slipper – these dainty flowers symbolize the Virgin Mary's Visitation to Elizabeth.

Lily – Lilies have long been recognized as symbols of purity and virginity and are associated with the Annunciation. A lily shown with thorns represents the Immaculate Conception. The lily is also a symbol of chastity. Saints:
Mary

Joseph
St. Clare
St. Kateri Tekakwitha
St. Catherine of Siena
St. Anthony of Padua
St. Rosalita of Parma
St. Joan of Arc (the fleur-de-lis)
St. Dominic
St. Casimir of Poland

Lily of the Valley – These tiny flowers represent chastity, and humility, and the Virgin Mary.

Marigolds – Another symbol of Mary, the marigold represents divine grace, purity, and maternal protection.
Our Lady of Guadalupe

Palm Branch – This flowerless branch represents martyrdom. Saints:
St. Sebastian
St. Agnes
St. Thecla

Pansy – Pansies represent remembrance and

meditation and are often used in funeral Masses. Saints:
St. Charles

Passionflower – Each part of the flower represents a different aspect of the Passion. The flower symbolizes the Crucifixion.
St. Gemma Galgani

Poinsettia – This Christmas flower represents the love of Christ and is often called the *Christmas Rose*.

Rose – Roses are most often associated with the Virgin Mary as they are a symbol of purity and virginity. Red roses represent martyrdom. A garland of roses is typically associated with the Rosary. A wreath of roses represents Heavenly joy. Many saints are symbolized by the rose:
Mary
St. Therese of Lisieux
St. Rose of Viterbo
St. Rita of Cascia
St. Rosalita of Parma
St. Elizabeth of Hungary

St. Cecelia
St. Dorothy
St. Rose of Lima

Snowdrop – These small, white flowers represent hope, purity, and virtuousness. Saints:
Mary
St. Brigid
St. Therese of Lisieux

Tulips – White tulips represent the Holy Spirit and are a symbol of forgiveness.
St. Rose of Viterbo

Violet – Violets symbolize humility and chastity. Saints:
Mary
St. Fina (also known as St. Seraphina)
St. Germain

About the Authors

Amy Schisler is an author, speaker, catechist, and pilgrimage leader. Amy's novels have won numerous literary awards. She lives on the Eastern Shore of Maryland where she and her husband raised three daughters. When she's not writing, Amy can usually be found on the Chesapeake Bay, hiking in the Rocky Mountains, or playing with her granddaughter.

Judy MacWilliams grew up in Southern Maryland near St. Clement's Island where her ancestors arrived in 1634. Most of her relatives were watermen and farmers. Married to Richard for over sixty years, they have three children, Amy, Scott, and Mike. Judy worked for the government and in education and wrote articles for several newspapers, including the Catholic Standard. Judy loves reading, gardening, and staying involved with her growing family that now includes seven grandchildren and one great-grandchild!

For more about the authors:
http://amyschislerauthor.com
http://psalm91min.com
http://facebook.com/amyschislerauthor
http://instagram.com/AmySchislerAuthor
https://www.goodreads.com/amyschisler

By Amy Schisler:

Novels

A Place to Call Home
Picture Me
Whispering Vines

The Good Wine
Summer's Squall
The Devil's Fortune

Chincoteague Island Trilogy

Island of Miracles
Island of Promise
Island of Hope

Chincoteague Sunsets Trilogy

Seeking Tranquility
Seeking Sugar and Spice
Seeking Space and Time

Buffalo Springs Series

Desert Fire, Mountain Rain
Under the Summer Moon
Sapphires in Snow

Rescuing the Rain Man

Children's Books

Crabbing With Granddad
The Greatest Gift

Spiritual Books and Bible Studies

Stations of the Cross Meditations for Moms (with Anne

Kennedy, Susan Anthony, Chandi Owen, and Wendy Clark)

A Devotional Alphabet

Meet the Saints from A-Z, A Children's Introduction to the Saints

Clothed With Strength and Dignity: Women of the Bible

Coming Soon:

A Very Loud Christmas (a book for children)